Compulsions of Silkworms and Bees

Julianna Baggott

Compulsions of Silkworms and Bees

Lena-Miles Wever Todd Poetry Series
PLEIADES PRESS
Warrensburg, Missouri
& Rock Hill, South Carolina

ISBN 978-0-8071-3256-2

Published by Pleiades Press
Department of English & Philosophy
The University of Central Missouri
Warrensburg, Missouri 64093
&
Department of English
Winthrop University
Rock Hill, South Carolina 29733

Distributed by Louisiana State University Press

Cover design by David G. W. Scott
Cover photograph by Steve Cole

2 4 6 8 9 7 5 3 1
First Pleiades Press Printing, 2007

Many of these poems appeared previously in *Arts & Letters, Green Mountains Review, Indiana Review, Margie, Melic Review, The Southeast Review, Southern Poetry Review, The Southern Review, Tin House, Third Coast, TriQuarterly, Virginia Quarterly Review, Washington Square,* and *Women's Studies Quarterly.* "Poetry Despises Your Attempts at Domesticity" was anthologized in *Sweeping Beauty* (University of Iowa Press). "Poem for a Friend Who Has Lost His Sanity" was read on NPR's *Talk of the Nation.*

Financial Assistance for this project has been pro-
vided by the Missouri Arts Council, a state agency.

This book is dedicated to the Reader and the Critic.

Man...produces philosophies and poems in about the same way silkworms produce cocoons and bees their hives.

—Hyppolyte Taine

Contents

One

Direct Address: Dear Reader,

I think of you more often than you think of me.
In fact, breath-hot, covetous, I've fallen in love with you,
the way you take up this burden, light-hearted, hopeful,
and tote it,
            your eyes hitching across the page.
And it's not just the idea of you, perfected
in polished recurring dream.
                                    No, I love the restlessness
of your corrupted soul, your heavy, murderous heart,
your infinite fascination with small shocking acts
of tenderness. I adore the lazy eye of your childhood,
that wistful yearning toward youth, the way
you sniff your food, suspiciously, before you eat it.

I know there are others for you, and I admit
sometimes my eye wanders toward that expanse
of sky, the beetle's polished back, a tulip bud
cracking as if broken before it blooms
and you lift from my mind, despite salting this ink.

But I always return to this moment, light
over one shoulder, the livingroom disheveled,
and your list of things to do. If you die first,
I will be the one thrown from the crowded church
for my wild, lustful mourning, for flailing, a gothic
moan and wail. Know that I want you to live forever,
not this little poem, this stiff altar of words, but you,
just now, golden and stewing in your hallowed beauty.

Dear Critic,

This pain is so familiar
(we were all children once)
I let it ride my back. I offer it in,
and I say, *Eat this plum,* fat and split,
some part of me, a sweet organ
—if not for you,
it will be left to the fruit flies,
that dizzy breath, that spot
of writhing shade.
I say, *Lie on this bed.*
I say, *I will sleep here*
                    next to you.
My blood will take comfort
in the sheets, will be loved
                    into the mattress
and years from now someone
will scrub the blood in the sun
and know only
that someone slowly died here.

1. Poetry Addresses Her Sister, the Novel

We're twins, but, in fact, I think my father wasn't yours—
newsman, bettor, drunk.
                        Do you recall the piano tuner,
how gently he slipped
                        the upright's lid back into its joints?
I admit we were identical once. No one could tell us apart
not even mother, sallow, harried, distracted
by wind, sun, the tuner
so often at the door that our piano sang always in perfect pitch.
As children we were called,
more often than not,
                        by the other's name.
But then you developed a swagger, busty with hips.
Mother preached to me, "Don't relish, don't romance disaster.
Don't grow inward so: Be more like your sister."
But I think even she would admit
                                you go on too much.
You need to learn to whittle soap
                                to a narrow bone, to live in steam
so the wool shrinks to a toughened swatch,
not a sweater, not a mitten, something otherworldly.
                        Why do you want so much?
I say little, but my memory is stained so deeply
                                it glitters.
You can't even recall how we used to fool mother
until she would make us
                        lift our skirts to reveal
the one birthmark, *mine*, a spot of night on my thigh.

2. The Novel Responds to Her Sister, Poetry

It isn't as easy as you'd think
to take the reader's hand, hang his hat
on the rack, to offer a seat.
Manners. I pass around tea and cakes.
Have you ever allowed these comforts?
You let them wander rooms, disoriented.
You invite them into the kitchen
so they can watch you sharpen knives.
Who wants to see your birthmark? Your scars?
I believe in constructs, the bridge,
but allow me the air around it.
I can recall more, truer.
The piano tuner, for example, was a sweet fag.
Our mother loved him. Our father,
yes, *ours*, ran into the tuner once in a bar
after our mother was dead.
The tuner told me this.
(I keep track of everyone I've ever met.)
Our father was no brute.
He walked the tuner to his car, asked
to see his bag of instruments, leather and bulky
as an old doctor's who makes house calls.
See, you know none of this, nothing.
The tuner tapped the fork, held it buzzing
to our father's ear. And the newsman, the bettor,
the drunk offered him a tender kiss.

Poetry Despises Your Attempts at Domesticity

The vacuum's one lung stiffens, aged,
it puffs too tightly.
                    It needs rest, Poetry says.
God bless her insistence: *Ignore your aunts,*
their plumage, their hospital corners, bleached
toilet bowls. The house aches. It has no gleaming
underside. It wants you to see it
for what it is, not for what it needs.
                  And what is it? You've forgotten.
A collection of smeared prints, the daily rigor
of staying, a blessing of dust.
And now you remember what the house was to you
as a child: a giant full-skirted woman, it gathered you in,
squatted like a nesting bird, loved you with its hovering vigilance.
And you loved it, heated duct work, squealing pipes,
because it could always stand, walk away, revealing you
and your family for what you are,
a knot, huddled, bare,
                  a circle of pale backs turned to the cold.

Q and A: How is it that poems can just fail? (the abridged version)

The poem can suffer a buoyed listing,
like a swamped canoe;

poor planning—
hitting an iceberg and not enough life boats;

or tidiness, hazardous symmetry,
an initial attempt at the St. Louis Arch off
by damning inches.

The poem can become so fearful and tidy
that it wraps itself in plastic slip covers.

The poem can marry Yoko Ono.

It can fail by doing its job,
as if this is someone's idea of work.

It can crow too loudly and pop something vital.

It can topple on its own Elvis image
until it's fat and working Vegas in studs.

The poem can whisper to itself, referring only
to the most intimate cataclysms.

It can hang itself with the golden rope
of one perfect line.

Q and A: Do you write about real stuff
or do you make it all up?

I would like to say that I invented
how darkness sometimes twists

into light, heats the dust motes till they are a million flares,
fragile chests of fire. I would like to say

that I had no mother
            but seemed to know just the same

the cool hand of love to fever, that I've never
spit or hummed or hated. I would like to say that

my brain is a little god churning out creation,
                        not the addled priest

who wakes up each morning, picks up his wicker basket
to fill with every dirty thing he finds,

who spends his nights hunched over silver polish,
                        buttons and spoons.

Even now, can't you hear
the clicking bones of my unlit, hissing strokes?

The Orphan Poem

I gave it up because I was too young,
too wild, unsuited to tending to its needs,
and it was needy, squalling, and I was tender,

needy myself. And so there was a basket,
and a gentle sea, or maybe there was a basket
and a bell and a darkened doorstep.

I cannot remember. But now I want it back,
because I'm older. I've matured,
steadied, found a rope in my body

and knotted it till it was taut. It has stayed taut.
More or less. I'm the only one
who can inform the poem of its genetic weaknesses

for drink, for sentiment, for longing.
And it is mine after all, just like me,
only smaller and more promising.

For Theodore Roethke

This house is filled with bodies,
the purring motors of chests and lungs.
The children—
      blurred cheeks, fevered—
rattle through winter and burn
      more fiercely than the boiler.
The hamster sheds and curls into its own loose fur
      as the humidifier pouts steam
and we dream of trains or teeming
fish-swirled streams.
         Sometimes I cannot sleep
with all this wheezing.
I churn the house, room to room to room,
keeping watch over these lips
      pursed, unpursed,
      drawn, fat, how they often seem
      perched on a single word
      chrysanthemum, rose
this garden of our fragile breathing.
It is a vigil like yours as a boy staying all night
in your father's greenhouse noting light on snow.
Come morning mine will swim up
with a slow gulping of air and sun
(blooming) their dizzy bobbing sway.

Q and A: Where do you get your ideas? Answer #1

I'm afraid of truth. Once it's given
it becomes a gift.
       Memory cannot remain pure memory
once spoken.
          My grandfather told me how it felt
before the amputations to have his dead legs float
in the tub, not his own after all, only bones, flesh.

Memory can be pulled up like a bloodstain pinking
under the cold press of water. The story is now my memory:
dark purple scars, bloated knees, white flaccid feet surface-risen.

How can he not remember just a little less?
I'd prefer to give away the replica, not a bit of the soul,
to turn the truth in my hand like a globed village snow-blurred.

But poetry demands the soul, and once you give it over, how easy
it becomes, an addiction to something like peeling fruit,
a simple disease, because ideas are simple.

You don't think, you listen. In the morning, I walk outside.
At once, the soul heaves and parts. Everything is talking,
even the rooted irises tonguing air.

Two

Q and A: Where do you get your ideas? Answer #2

Here it rises slowly from the fire of a burning day,
the poem lifts, frayed, ashen, bristling orange.
                                        Smoking.
The poem begins again, *again,* as memory:
My mother sprays starch in the basement,
                    the zigzagging iron, the cloud of steam.
And I can feel the give of the board's metal legs,
the quick heavy collapse, before I prop and wedge it
upright in the spot next to the drier.
This moment has nothing to do with today—
my husband behind the wheel, turning left
onto Main from Haines.
He asks about a roll of stamps, prices up a penny.
I shift, and he knows I'm struck. *What is it?* he asks.
I say, *A poem,* as if it's Aunt Dorris on the corner waving,
or a cop diverting traffic up ahead, or this:
not my mother shining with sweat, not so much
the moth-tinging bulb above her head,
                            but the poem, in the road
hissing like a rearing hood-flared cobra, the old sibilant iron,
                            its red glowing eye.

The Current Events Poem:
The Hindenburg and Twin Towers

The radio announcer admitted to drizzle as the majestic airship,
a bloated shark, glided in. But the dirigible was a doomed idea, overall.
Fire, a raining now of parts—bodies, metal, ash, a hull of flame—
thirty-four seconds, and the announcer never stopped talking.
His voice cracked. He was crying. He knew immediately
the wide historical landscape, uttered, *Oh, the humanity.*

        I would have been the oddity who stood
beneath the umbrella, unmoving, caught by the spectacle,
my view as small as a pinprick in a homemade camera.
I would have walked around for months, saying, *Yes, I was there.*
The fire was hot.

        Don't look to me for this. I have nothing to say
except remember that summer, we worried about sharks
slipping closer to shore. I slept better after the crashing planes,
thinking, no, it won't be sharks. It won't be anything we can avoid.

Q and A: Do you have any tips? Answer #1

I suggest a greedy heart, an appetite for hoarding.
Recall the two brothers whose house collapsed under the strain
of lifelong collection?

      Imagine the second floor creaking laboriously,
like a ship deck, the horn a wheezing lung, before it buckles and gives.
I like to believe they held hands as they had before jumping off

the cement pool's edge wearing handmade trunks which matched,
not only each other's but their kitchen curtains, the love-seat pillow.
(Frugality is a family trait.)

If they'd had enough time, before the house's last heaving breath,
they could have found the pillow, the curtains, each suit,
                                    newspaper-wrapped
as if fragile, in a box marked "summer, 1949," and within the stitches,
their mother's hands.

      Who would give that away?
You must not only understand the brothers,
their broken, blood-bruised, fatty bodies dug from the rubble,

      but the boys they were. Take them in on a given afternoon,
play the neighbor who troubles over their wiry mother, buzzing
                                    the boys' heads
so close with the clippers she leaves nicks that scab,
and collects the fine loose hairs to stuff a pillow.

      Invite them in. Let them warm up to the cat.
Set out cookies on napkins which they will wrap,
half-eaten and keep forever. It's tricky. This keeping.
Don't let them see your daughter.

Q and A: Do you simultaneously submit?

My grandfather sold Electroluxes in Morgantown
door-to-door under the constant rain of ash.

A laboring mountain town, it was a joke
to think of keeping it clean.

Roadside wild flowers pinched coal.
Soot snuck in to gray the sugar bowl,

to dust baseboards, wash tubs, porch gliders,
the bird's newspaper-lined cage, the bird, its clawed feet.

His boss had a pork-pink face, jowls.
He drove the men around town in a converted hearse,

dropping them at street corners. Glowering,
he'd say, "No tea cakes. Cover your beat."

Now I am the boss in the long black car and, too,
my grandfather at the top of High Street, dusk;

he'll disappear one night, drunk, die in a hospital
in upstate New York, his head wrapped like a swami,

but for now he's sober. He says, "No tea cakes.
Cover your beat, Baggott. Keep at it."

A family to feed, who would knock once and
sit on a single stoop through the bitter winter?

In a warm parlor, he'll prove the vacuum's power
by sucking up a metal ball which locks to the tube's mouth.

I admit I have no tricks, only the hearse and the heavy case,
a slouch and shuffle, a valley of lit windows.

Poetry as the Nurse You've Come to Rely On

Poetry loiters around tragedy. She likes the smell
of astringent, the hospital an epic in its architecture
                                                of suffering.
She adores how the rooms,
            white and exact in their spare simplicity,
are like words lining, breaking,
the repetition of room after room.
I'd prefer not to think of my uncle's sugary blood,
my grandmother's stubborn, stricken arteries,
my cousin's dying child,
                            but Poetry is making her rounds,
a swish of skirt, a rub, rub of stockinged thighs.
She reports: *They will all have to labor. Death*
will be born here, limp and sallow.
The clipboard offers a sense of duty, formality,
but cannot hide her grieving air.
I despise the poem rising, the way she hands it over—
like a scrawled prescription
                            for treating misery—
but I thank her for it, zip it into my pocketbook
and drive home too slowly, too carefully,
checking the seatbelt's click and hold, the rearview mirror's
steady backward eye, the radio for its ardent promise
                                    of inclement weather.

Q and A: Why don't you write formal poetry?

I cannot help it. I mistake quatrain for Coltrane,
terza rima for tiramisu. Poetry is horns. It tastes sweet.
Anapest is made with basil; and dactyl rolls up,
all tongue-muscle and jelly, onto beaches.
It's comforting to some, this erector set of tools,
this tidiness, as if the world can be arranged.
And I agree there is desperation in numbers,
an attempt to keep account like naming babies
in an orphanage. But I will forever 1-2-3
a waltz. Each rhyme is a bell-ting from my days
in a butcher shop, someone wanting lunch meat.
I prefer this delusion: a Petrarchan sonnet—
silk-lined, fitted, a bishop's hat, tall and black
with red piping—I wear it on my fat head.

Q and A: How do your children affect your work?

          This morning at the kitchen table,
my three-year-old son drew a picture of me:
so much swollen head, stick-arms poking out of my ears,
stick-legs under my chin, three dots for eyes and nose,
a mouth-line, a scribble of hair,
              and swirling away, unconnected,
two circles, he told me, one for pee, one for poop.
I was concerned. *Where's the house?* I asked.
                  The grass? Where are you?
It's morning, he told me. *It just got done snowing.*
I'm watching you.
And for a moment it was like that:
           I am standing in a trackless field,
wondering how I got here, how long I've been standing
mute, deaf, possibly blind with my big head, dot eyes,
and slanted, shut mouth, a perfect likeness.
          How could I not have seen myself before?

An Ars Poetica about Ars Poetica

I dislike the metaphor, the incubation of art, the labor, birth.
No one ever advises the pregnant woman,
"It's like writing a poem. Bear down and breathe."
It would be more truthful to say we pull art from our sleeves
like magicians do rabbits. A narrow squeeze, a tug, quick hands,
and then, ta da! the poem flops open, ears and feet, blinks
almost pink eyes, twitches, alive.

My husband and I tried to tell the children, honestly.
We began with sperm and egg, trudged through
penis, vagina, uterus, tried to skip
insertion, but nailed with a furrowed brow, a *how*,
mumbled through what we never thought of before
as a technicality. It's not easy to marry science and love,
much less the quarreling threesome that art makes.
Poems aren't made, so much as found. We began again:

Remember how we lost you once
in the science institute's walk-through heart? Hot, airless,
the muscle thrumming over an invisible intercom, we traced
the narrow stairs, running our hands along the tight red walls.
Your voices somewhere up ahead, echoed off chambers,
and we called you by name, louder and louder
until the heart was a bell and with hard shakes
we rang it. One by one you came running.

For Charles Simic

Today, at the community pool,
my fists are the heads of birds
and I want them to open their dead eyes,
their wings, to sail off from these lank arms,
this loveless heart…to beat and beat
above our heads,
mothers around the pool, rubbing lotion
into the pink skin of morning lessons.
Her fists opened and became birds,
that's what they will say to their husbands
tonight, if they dare.
                Her fists became birds
and most will sleep with their hands
pinned under their soft stomachs, but one,
perhaps two
        will lie like the living dead,
hands crossing their chests,
                inviting the birds to rise.

Q and A: Don't poets just write the same poem over and over?

We stand in the pool, rings of small waves
bounce out from our waists, spread,
the old woman and me, our circles colliding.
Her groove-stuck needle is *babies,* is *welcome,*
is *I hope you will be as happy here as we have.*
I will not be so lucky. My brain will stop on an ugly note
to hold, hold, metronome ticking. As it is,
I've been told my obsessions: I don't need much,
a bucket, sudsy for mopping, and a character,
morose or only neglectful, will drown.
And if it isn't the inching in of water,
then death, a peaceful candle, will find
a silk robe's gaping sleeve, catch, flare.
I will not welcome. I'll caution: *Keep your babies*
from the boiling rice pot, the blue ring of lit gas.
I hope you will be as mindful here as we have,
and that ticking—it is no metronome.

Three

Q and A: Why do you write? Answer #1

Because my heart never understood biology.
The nuns wouldn't allow us to dissect God's creatures;
there were no preserved pig fetuses, no thawed worms,
no sharp knives. We had books, the heart splayed
                              on open pages.
And I memorized, repeated the words until
                        they were not themselves.

Coronary, coronary the heart's reed horn.
Vena Cava, Vena Cava, a night club singer in a beaded gown.
Atrium, atrium, a glass room filled with birds.

Imagine them all, as I did, filling my chest.

But now I worry about overcrowding.
Vena and the birds and the horn are gone.
And still is there enough room for all of you?
My heart has become
                a crawlspace,
and I see the packed-in bodies, rows of faces,
                              no light, no air.
Tomorrow will it shrink
          to the size of a table-top aquarium?
And soon will it be a muscle fitting neatly
in my chest? It is my worst fear:
a heart the exact size and shape of a heart.

The Workshop Poem

I prefer mutations. Wild flowers edit, revise.
There is a time to let poems breed, dirty, rooted
                              among surly weeds.
(It's ugly, no doubt. The weeds outnumber the flowers.
And the weeds are always right, even when they disagree
                              which they always do.)
I hope for bees, the crosshatching zigzag.
Perhaps, for a while, it might seem
there's growing uniformity, a blurred
                    solid-colored patch of ground,
but watch—Darwin is clapping, breathless—
just when you begin to think that the outcome is knowable,
that the flowers always nudge up, untwist, dilate
at the moment you expect dilation,
        watch the barren stem, a weed, in fact,
                         suddenly littered with buds, burst
a profusion of orange wings—
what to do?—a fire in the flower bed.

The Stolen Poem: My Brother Poem
after Levine's "What Work Is"

He won't admit to rain,
only a break in the sun to wait out.
For now, a mist. His kids slip through the park gate,
Almost old, my brother's blond whitens.
Work doesn't exist, only a hearty laugh, damp grass.
He forgets everything but the children, the gate,
for a moment, a shift of sentimentality.
He has five kids—he should be toughened—but his eyes mist,
the risen blur of love.
I see him now, from a distance,
his ruddy cheeks, sloppy pants, chins, tinged mustache.
Unlike other men who turn sour, joyless,
who narrow to a staircase soul,
he grins, beams, a search-light,
and, too, the stubborn ulcer hidden,
his refusal of anger alive and livid,
the pooled sting of sleepless hours.
Saturday, it will lead somewhere.
My brother will wait for it to unwind
amid the no-no of children, jazz, scotch.
He won't play the hired man today.
He reasons loneliness the opposite of love,
asks for company, stands joyful, sings in a crowd,
a flooding love. He swells with it.
Once he traveled beside bluesmen,
far from home, the sour stink of reeds, horns,
hotel sheets. It became a miserable moan of sax.
He hitched a ride in a Cadillac, east,
recalls now only the old German on trumpet,
his jowly face pursed to bawl. Hours turn,
Saturday, an opera he doesn't try to understand.
He hates to read: It invents a different world,
and he always prefers his own. But music,
oh, how it moves beside you, within,
shoulders the day. He doesn't close

his eyes to it, but allows its kiss.
A simple benediction. An obvious gift.
He is no longer young and dumb.
His meanness has atrophied to a splinter of bone.
Incapable of drifting beyond,
he adores all of us, this presence,
because we are and he is.

Q and A: Do you think it helps your poetry if you've had
    a lot of experiences and have seen the world?

It helps to have a room, a window with many panes.
From there you can see the neighbor's slippered feet
beneath the porch glider, a planter, the brittle heads
of a dead mum, surrounded by miniature flags.
You can hear the eave's lone, raucous hive.
Inside, a box fan.
                    Pare down. Stop here
with this one hand, its paint stains, veins, the missing tip
of a forefinger. This nub with its stunted nail—notwithstanding
the sparrow, its darting climb and clamp to line—
is enough to tell everything
anyone has ever wanted to know.

The Exercise-Born Poem, A Test-Tube Baby

We are each a country with our own anthem,
and I adore the border of your soul,
this familiar crossing an outpost with weeds.
I linger here at the brittle fence
                    held strong by undergrowth.
I can see through the trees, a lake reflecting sun.
From the gatehouse,
there's always a radio squawking—
a static-garbled ball game.
And the border guard
sometimes catches his reflection
in the window's glare; once a pugilist,
he takes a stance, fists, keen eyes,
bandy legs,
                    but usually he dozes,
gun handle popping from a belt
cinched around loose uniform slacks,
his bullet sash sags
        sweet as a beauty pageant queen.
When I tap, he startles,
and I adore his lazy passport stamping,
the way he says,
        Enjoy. Take what's yours.
                    It's all yours.

Eve Recalls Birthing and Her Discovery of Metaphor

My baby's purple head newly wrung of blood
reddened. Adam rubbed his body dry, no longer fish-like,

while I fisted my own stomach, to push out
the shining clots as dark red as bruised, ground-rotting apples,

my stomach, too, like the softened fruit, the way only the skin
    holds shape
when the inside has turned to meal. My belly dull-colored,

almost gray and empty, I was the first to see how one thing
stands sadly for another, emotion mingling sweetly,

cruelly with the world. I knew what it was to be
not free, but freed from, to be the garden left behind,

not just the willow, but all the sagged limbs weeping.

Q and A: Why do you write? Answer #2

I am obsequious. The world a bitch,
lording it all over us, the press
                    of clouds,
the loud sun, and how we must march on
with the heavy jostle
                    of meat and blood,
milk and brine.
Everything you touch leaves a stain,
even simple pollen, a bright
                              too-cheery yellow.
And each person
          is a world, a bitch lording,
and when I see one work a button
into a hole,
my heart catches, a tinderbox fire,
and I say, *Look at us.*
                    Just look at us.

On the Personal Poem: In Defense of Rotting
for Robert Pack, upon the occasion of his misunderstanding of Yeats

"Yeats stated the…idea more bluntly: 'All that is personal soon rots.'
The artist must emphasize the ongoing life of his species rather than
his or her own individuality… If anything remains, it will be what Yeats
calls 'monuments of unaging intellect.' The attempt to cling to an
assertion of the self is a form of the denial of death and the inability
to accept the ephemerality of nature."
—Robert Pack on Yeats and Pack's sequence of poems *Rounding it Out*.

Ah, Mr. Pack—the old poet's sperm churn like warm honey,
that one spot in his body perfectly preserved,
always seventeen and swimming like an otter.
A man can believe some things will never spoil,

but, truth, everything is washed away by blood,
even their stone-white, cock-straight monuments
of unaging intellect. So why not say my mother,
my country, my tongue, my bread and cup,

my bright red cells brimming? All mine.
I throw myself into the rot, breathing
the dark breath of the body, my bones
drying up even in this thick soup.

Give me the poem like the fuck you come up from,
breathless, this life as death, eggs ticking away,
almost rusted shut, stolen into
by tail-flicking thieves, deathly breeding.

Poem for Dean Young

There have been mistakes in your logic,
too many to catalogue, but here are a few.
When you're vacuuming, you hear music, yes,
but it is, in fact, me: Julianna Baggott, singing
one of those songs about someone taking
somebody else to a place they've never been before,
but I sing my own lyrics: you, Dean Young,
take me to a place I've been many times,
thought I knew too well, and don't want to return to.
An abbreviated list of locales: the grocer's slow lobster tank,
the airplane cabin before take-off where I'm aware
of my selfish relief as the flight attendant instructs
place the oxygen mask over your own mouth first
before assisting others, my therapist's office
where she demands I gauge anxiety on a scale of 1 to 10
(right now I am at a solid 7), and my childhood kitchen,
how a flower crown preserved in the fridge
is a cold bite on the head. (Now 8 and rising.)
(My husband says parentheses are a sign of weakness.
My mother claims it's bad posture. I'm too exhausted
and hunched to comment.) And when
you put your ear to grocery stock,
it isn't the paper towels crying, but me: Julianna Baggott,
and I'm saying, please, Dean Young, do not
write a poem about this shopping trip
or if you must then write it on a piece of paper
you wouldn't mind eating.
Or better yet write the poem on your hand,
your arm (if long) your chest (if epic)
and then take a hot, sudsy shower, because
(anxiety rating: 9) Jimi Hendrix opened for The Monkees
for seven days in December of 1966 and while
searching for that information I found an article
that said: *Penile sheaths of the 16th century*

were dullingly thick, made from animal guts
and fish membranes in addition to linen,
because, fuck, it's all your fault that from now on
it'll be like this. You silly jackass nincompoop,
I am falling in love with your perversity
and I would desperately prefer something else (10!);
actually, let me clarify: nearly anything else at all.

The Poem that Wants to be Written

It's a risen dick, how, so blood-cocked it lolls heavily
toward any other heat,

                and the bridesmaids' taffeta dresses
bustled to giant pink rump bows, a row of them,
that's the world calling out,

                everything bedecked;
the rain, you say, is leaf-ticking; it could be a poem, couldn't it?
This has nothing to do with words,

           or love, for that matter, only an urging
toward release, to lift one's head from it,
to reel, still ringing, only to cast out

           again, a wild eye, the clatter-roll of language,
fever-pitched, your chest a struck-gong,
as the sound lifts, it still shivers. *More.*

Concerning Mr. Frank O'Hara and his Critics, the Assassins in his Orchards

In my family, the sweet madam
sends whores into the orchards

to lure assassins inside. Murderers
in our beds. It's okay, I whisper, to hate me,

to love me, to hate me.
Oh, critic, be ignorant, be insolent,

and be sour! Unlike Mr. O'Hara,
I have no need to live forever.

Four

Prose Poem: I Send Poetry a Postcard

It's burning hot here in the square with its oversized grill-work clock, rumpled pigeons, its school children gathered around the sea turtle who wandered up from the beach. His tiled back as shiny as a sun dial, he sometimes peers out of his shell, one wrinkled eye, surprised to find himself here, ancient but alive and well. Airplanes pass overhead, the shining silver buzz of them, and don't you remember bombings? Weren't you the redheaded child the others wouldn't run with because they thought you a bright easy target? You said that the sky once was a swarm of metal bees. I don't miss you, but sometimes I think…if only you were here, if only you could see how at night we all glow from within, wicked and bright as jack-o-lanterns, as if we swallowed fire. I'm sure you would have something to say, I can nearly hear you: *souls, torches.*

Poetry Punishes You for Your Absence

She's not an easy lover who simply tilts her head
when you appear on the front stoop.

Will she allow the porch light to cast heavenly redemption
like a bare bulb in a church-basement Christmas pageant?

No, there's scowling, silence. And when finally
she takes you to the tub to wash away the world's filth,

you're always shocked, no matter how many times
you've strayed, that she doesn't gently cup your head,

but dunks it, again and again,
a baptism that just won't take.

The Poem of Thanksgiving: I am Writing Again

God bless the shrunken roots
                     once again tuberous, fruitful.
A complex multiplication of cells,
                      a rice grain bloats to the size of a boot.
Everything barbed hitches. The angels bow.
                      The light switch hums, poorly wired.
It could spark.
                      The neck is stretched, pale, blood blue.
There may be rhyme as garish as an orange lily,
                      lewd, cocking its stamen,
but call off the funeral, undress the pall-bearers,
hang up their dark suits so the pleats keep, unshave
each face.
                      The umbrella was broken,
but the button clicks and its spidery legs pop into place.

The Poem that Surfaces on a Bad Day Among Giants

Let's call it a fish, a clichéd trout, because sometimes
I can only muster the store-bought version of poetry, like this:
the fish twists just beneath the surface, (No, this isn't Bishop)
gives a glint, shows its mirrored scales (Here, not Rilke either),
and passes through my rooted thigh-high waders
(newly ordered from LL Bean? Pack would say no:
Shouldn't poetry remain timeless? And wasn't he talking to Yeats?)

It disappears.

I cast and cast, the same perforated worm,
and let's face it, the hook is old and rust-mottled.
(The Neo-Realists want the hook, only, not my brain.)
It stains my fingers.
         But the fish is perfected
by its absence. (If only this poem had gills,
hinged spokes, could breathe water...)
But I stand and stand, scanning the lake for ripples,
knowing that if I'm patient, the fish will one day,
   out of sympathy, out of pure despair,
drive the barbed tip into its jaw
                  to let me think I've hooked it.

A Caution Against Historical Poetry
in the Voice of Lazarus

I would have said, *Don't unearth me.*
But I was brought back to life, or think of it this way:
I have the painful distinction of dying twice.
The living! Tediously selfish. I don't blame Jesus.
He didn't expect the crowd of mourners,
Martha and Mary wrung out from weeping.
He was still naive about our humanness, our vast capacity
not always for love, but grief.
            He recalled the story of the king
who killed himself by burning his castle to the ground,
and tried to understand again our need to take
everything with us, our instinct to guard, to keep.
But he was disoriented, thinking of all that had to be
undone.
        Sorrow doesn't fold in on itself like water.
Guilt must be returned, poured back
                 like blood into the body.
The son must become a son again, shrinking to the edges,
and the wife, *my wife,* aged by grief, had to be pressed clean.
Alone in the cave, my first breath was an outward gust,
not the drawing in of new air. My lungs sighed out
what I'd died holding tight.
I stood, wearily. I did what the dead always do:
                I followed the light.
They pushed the rock away from the tomb
and I appeared, wrapped in wax-stiff clothes.
Jesus said, *Untie him. Set him free,* but into what world?
My wife doesn't complain, but the stench of death never fades.
Long after Jesus climbed into heaven,
I was left with what? My desire for the tight fit of a shroud,
            the silent tomb of clean memory.

Termites: A Caution on Love Poetry

If the love poem suffers softness
                    like weathered cedar,
termites will swarm, burrow, fatten.
If, for example, a widow flowers
with newfound passion, make sure
she's chopping the head off a fish
and the fish
                    should be pregnant,
spilling eggs like an orange blossom.
If the widow simply flowers, all believability is lost,
and you can poke a pencil into a support beam.
The innards are airy,
                    held together by paint.
The widow, don't forget, is a hardened slave
to her home.
          Toughen, she'd tell you herself.
She understands love and the best way
to kill termites—suffocation:
                    powder and an airtight house.

Marriage as Creative Process, a Love Poem

Let's marry again, this time as metaphor:
I'll be the idea of love and you can be
                              the curtains, breathing.
Allow me this: every day is a proposal,
an acceptance.
            Marriage is a reckless aperture,
the sudden floods and fades of light.
            No, you can be the idea of love
and I will be
            the curtains, breathing.
A moment can halt us, turn us round.
We can lose our bearings in the dim kitchen
worn from our own bare feet.
            There is no idea of love,
only the curtains breathing.
But we're smart
                        to be so doggedly messy,
leaving our hearts everywhere.
I reach for an apple and it begins
                        to click, to beat.

Poetry as a Lover

I know what you expect. Sentimentality.
Double blurred vision,
       your lover twinning from romance. No.
This is a short contest of desire. She won't spend the night.
Poetry shrugs off foreplay, says, *No thank you*
to the languorous cigarette, says, *The poem is orgasm.*
Page after page, I work harder than any stunt cock porn star.
And yet within,
        time erodes. The day washes away.
Canyons rise, layer upon layer.
The wind shaves
      a mountain. Stones smooth.
Even the ancient bayou swamps slide in
            from nowhere.
Mosquitos form
      a singing screen. Heat,
the ache of dying. Prehistoric gators, now fearful, screw
their eyes down beneath bone.
          And, here,
Poetry finishes first.
      Nostrils glide, pinch, disappear.

Poetry as the Mother who Chooses Between Us
for Olena

It isn't a space but still we gather, pooling like blood
around the fractured bone of this.

                              Poetry is to blame.

What does she promise you?
I can only imagine how tender it is in the field.
The glass pane is warm, my hand spread to it.

With me, sometimes Poetry wrings her hands,
knowing my weakness for weakness. She pleads,
Stay with me. I don't like to be alone.

This would be fine but then she turns saccharin.
This would be fine but then she tells me
that I'm her favorite. It isn't true. Plainly.

              My thoughts connect, tail to trunk
like circus elephants. And I've fallen in love
with the reader, too, but not unconditionally.

As a child, I thought Poetry was drawn to dizzying hair,
madman brows, livid scar tissue. But now I recognize
the onset.

I'd like to think I can say it this way—
her nipples were once small, pink dollops,
rosy as dolly cheeks—and only you would understand.

But I'm a bastard child. I never suckled there.
I'm weak, my soul made of leather. Sometimes
you meet her in the hall and your bodies

glide not around, but through.
Look at her now, pretending to be a turban
and you wrap her gladly 'round your fucking head.

Five

In Response to *Poetry is a House with Many Rooms*

What optimism! How would we decide between
slate or tin, marble or linoleum?
Is there a tidy list—those of us who are not allowed
near the oven, the balcony, the locked garage?
And, damn it, I've been put in the room with the dog
locked up for leg-humping the guests.
Mr. Suarez has filled the bathroom with canaries—
now shit-stains and steam. Shapiro and Howe
have cluttered the livingroom with babbling relatives.
Mr. Howard is wallpapering with love letters, again,
and Frost has let the apples go to rot, but they are barely seen
through Merwin's constant mist.
And oh God! The European slide shows, the endless jazz!
And the shushing
            each time someone enters a room!
Over the shushing alone, we would hunt
for our disassembled guns, cordon off
our private wreckages, pace our perimeters.
No, no, this is no house,
            too many locks and keys.
The best we can hope for is a hotel-motel,
the walls as thin as Yellow Pages.
Occasionally, a phone rings.
A man coughs. The shower pipes groan.
And at night, there are only the sounds of
fucking and dying and fucking.

Apologia for my Obsessions

I apologize for my obsessions, in particular:
memory, hissing, things that beat, tick, click,
flowering, swelling, weeding, and the body's decay.
I have become self-conscious like a girl with a hefty bosom
who sleeps at night in a tightened bra.
But oh how the hissing weeds are the world's utterances—
the orchid's delicate ticking tongue, the clicking throats
of crows, and my own body beating
against this boy and that. Flower, swell, the world
puffed on air, lung-tight and rising.
How is it that each time, after a poem
or this memory of ancient sex,
I cannot walk for all the littered dead?

An Apologia for Using Words in Poetry

Words—how we fasten and ratchet them to meaning.
Fearless as soldiers, righteous and equine

                                        as queens,
we work them.
            I have muscled my way through—written
like a bike messenger through a field of stubbled corn
from word to meaning and back, bell clamped to handlebar.

Let the words crawl and burrow and wheeze in dusty air.

Let them bawl and fume and flower. I've spent hours, years
prying their stubborn muscle-sealed shells.
            Do infants, do jungles, do wasps

                                    writhe within them?
The words arch and buck and I mistake this wildness
for something other than hatred.
                            When they hang in a line,
don't they abandon themselves, a resignation?
Words despise meaning, would shake free for the chance
to be snow, to be flour, to be,
            for once, a collection of sounds that works
the tongue and lips, to be not sifted and baked
                        into this tall proper upright cake.

Talking Dirty: The Marketing of Poetry

I'm drawn to the boy in the back row, enduring
          his girlfriend's artsy phase. Somewhere
there's a ball game. In fact, he's worn his cap,
a rebellion that earns him no points.
His weary slouch, his beaten dogginess—
I want to tell him I understand, and it's regrettable.
I prefer to ease him in, then make him want
what he didn't want before.
He's been taught associations, a bell and a biscuit.
He's weak (sex) for subliminal (sex) advertising.
And I will promise anything.
          He should be warned
I come from a long line of pool-hall hustlers,
snake oil salesmen and whores.
          In fact,
let's apply dancing girls to poetry,
          pop-top cakes and tassels.
It's worked for Buicks, by god,
and poets should choose lies more carefully.
I'm willing to admit we sometimes pretend to make sense,
that we are guilty of passing off incoherence as genius.
I'll play down Victorians, play up the Beats
if only for their rock-star personas.
If he asks, I'll tell him language poetry is,
more often than not, a naked emperor,
and "The Wasteland," finally I'll confess:
no one gets it.
          Tomorrow I'll disagree.
I'll vote for purity of purpose,
          but tonight
I'll tell him each stanza is a girl's ruffled bedroom
where you have appeared in twisted sheets,

(one day there will be a quarter-fed vibrating bed)
            and each line break
isn't a carriage return,
but a soft breath, a moan and sigh.

Argument with Louis Simpson

I was born to counter space, heating ducts,
that warm purr,
                    to gentle incubation, to waste
my life—if lucky enough—in the golden hum
of hours passing
                    and comfort.
But you deny the middle-class suburbanites
as the hive-work of bees drilling into trim.
Yes, we are born to it, as you say,
                                like those singing
in procession to the temple. Damn it, man,
look closer. Have you forgotten that
            you are a temple singing just as
            we are each a temple singing?

Poetry in the Suburbs

You taught me to choose the apple, every time;
perfection is monotonous,

boredom the most dangerous of moods—
remember sixteen, the roar

of tires as you did a topless backbend
out the window on the interstate? I envied

your yellow hair whipping, the blood-rush,
the way each car slowed to glimpse abandon.

      Luckily we cannot undo the bite
despite the attempts: L.A. and here in Delaware suburbs.

Sometimes there is no apple, no tree of knowledge,
no snake, and someone must invent them

like the Corvette, the cigarette,
the A-bomb.

The garden so sickly sweet in this well-mown hometown,
each morning glory so dutifully climbing its stake,

how could we live without longing,
regret, nostalgia.

I'm not so brave. To know good from evil,
you became the serpent, became the tree, the fruit.

      You hauled a slippery Eden—
of pool patios, card parties, stiff-cupped bras,

of sod, sweaty uncles, dark theaters,
the quiet stifled neighborly rape—

around on your back like a revolutionary
through the bowery with the dead body

of the king. I remember him well:
sweet, senile, blind, and deaf.

Q and A: Do you have any tips? Answer #2

How many times do I have to say it: Listen,
a whine in a bulb,
                              its hiss of life,
the fragile sister of mosquito, the electric life of wings.
There is a wheel rut for each of us somewhere.
Look closely at the skein of eggs,
                              root the mud for a clamped oyster
fallen from a truck. Cover your nose and mouth
with both hands, and there,
                                        in that shallow cup,
feel a buffalo's breathing steam.
A toppled stone, its face veiled by weeds—
crouch. The blooms become helmets.
Allow for delirium, a thirst. Take in
so much sun that you can feel a cold absence,
as if you've sipped a hole into the world.

The Place Poem: Sparrow's Point

I was told it was named for a man, Thomas Sparrow,
but too late, no matter. I've seen what was once here
before the blasts of tugs hauling barges, the bleating trains,
the rattling gusto of the Red Rocket streetcar,
before it was a company town steeped in fumes,
dwarfed by thick electric wires; before everything—
gutters, fenceposts, penny candies left to harden
in bowls—was coated in the steel mill's red dust,
before the dust, wet from the billowing steam
of boiler chimneys, became a clammy paste:
                              Singing trees.
Sparrows, thousands. Low-lying marshland
                              and yawning blue sky
filled suddenly with dart and turn.
The air had muscled current. The birds beat, glided.
Now ghosts, they have the power to pass
                              through us,
to lodge and pulse in our ribs.
Put your hand on my heart, *there, there, now,*
                              the livid flutter.

Q and A: When do you know a poem is done?
for Rodney Jones

I have said that each shirtless boy pumping a bike could be a lover,
that a new baby needs attending. There is no
                                              finish; only
a shift of attention.
                          Like this: I determine that it's spring.
An observation not of bright crocus beaks breaking ground from
below or rain,

but some clockwork,
                my whole body suddenly tightening with blood.

Sometimes, yes, forewarned by slow warming,
but usually it's as if winter were an old house in a field

torn down while I slept
                and I'm not sad that it's gone,

                                        but overwhelmed
by how much sky it had been holding back.

About the Lena-Miles Wever Todd Poetry Series

The editors and directors of the Lena-Miles Wever Todd Poetry Series select one book of poems for publication by Pleiades Press and Winthrop University each year. All selections are made blind to author-ship in an open competition for which any American poet is eligible.

Other Books in the Series

Snow House by Brian Swann (selected by John Koethe)
Motherhouse by Kathleen Jesme (selected by Thylias Moss)
Lure by Nils Michals (selected by Judy Jordan)
The Green Girls by John Blair (selected by Cornelius Eady)
A Sacrificial Zinc by Matthew Cooperman (selected by Susan Ludvigson)
The Light in Our Houses by Al Maginnes (selected by Betty Adcock)
Strange Wood by Kevin Prufer (selected by Andrea Hollander Budy)